Grab That Microphone
Your Guide to Becoming an In-Demand Podcast Guest

Christine Blosdale

DEDICATION

To the visionaries and trailblazers who boldly share their stories, wisdom, and passions through the power of podcasting:

Your voice resonates.
Your message inspires.
Your journey matters.

This book celebrates your courage, honors your authenticity, and fuels your relentless pursuit of dreams. May it empower you to amplify your unique voice and leave an indelible mark on the world.

For every aspiring podcast guest ready to make waves – this is your guide, your companion, your launchpad.

Dare to be heard.
Dare to make a difference.

With heartfelt gratitude,
Christine Blosdale, Podcast and Media Coach at
ChristineBlosdale.com

TABLE OF CONTENTS

ACKNOWLEDGMENTS

To my former and current clients and students:

Your trust, dedication, and enthusiasm have been the driving force behind this book. Your willingness to learn, adapt, and persevere has been truly inspiring.

Whether you've sought guidance for podcast appearances or ventured into creating your own shows, your passion for sharing knowledge and connecting with audiences has been a privilege to witness.

Each of you has left an indelible mark, reaffirming the transformative power of podcasting. Your successes, both big and small, have filled me with immense joy and pride.

Thank you for allowing me to be part of your journey.

Your commitment to your goals and the trust you've placed in me have been an honor.

You are, quite simply, amazing.

With heartfelt gratitude,
Christine

ABOUT THE AUTHOR, CHRISTINE BLOSDALE

With over 25 years of experience in Media and Coaching, Christine Blosdale stands out as a dynamic force in the industry. She's worked with global thought leaders, coaches, bestselling authors and social media influencers from around the world.

She's also a four-time #1 Amazon Bestselling Author, an Award Winning Media Personality and a featured contributor to America Online, The Microsoft Network, Woman's Day, Ticker News, Pacifica Radio, Take 5 Magazine and Hollywood.com.

If that wasn't enough, she's also the Producer and Host of two popular podcasts - The 5 Minute Micro Podcast on Podcasting and Out of The Box With Christine.

Christine's unique and fun coaching style has already helped hundreds of clients get the visibility and attention they deserve through podcasting. They are thrilled with the results - and you will be too!

As a radio professional Christine has produced The Roseanne Barr Radio Show, and has interviewed such notables as Marianne Williamson, Ralph Nader, John Paul DeJoria, Kelly Carlin, Wanda Sykes, John Trudell, Mariel Hemingway, Ed Asner, Meredith Baxter, Dr. Judith Orloff and Nobel Peace Prize laureate Wangari Maathai.

An all-in-one media coach you can trust, Christine has a solid reputation in the industry based on decades of experience.

To book a FREE consult visit ChristineBlosdale.com

Other books written by Christine Blosdale include;

Podcastonomics: Unlocking the Secrets of Profitable Podcasting for Beginners

Podcast Pro: A Step-by-Step Guide on How to Get Booked on Podcasts

Pod Your Way To Success: How To Use Podcasting As Your Marketing Superpower For Business

Christine Blosdale's Podcasting For Beginners Workbook: A Simple and Easy To Use Guide For New Podcasters

Your Amazing Itty Bitty Podcast Book: The top 15 Reasons Why You Need To Tap Into The Power (and Profits) of Podcasting

INTRODUCTION

Welcome to the world of podcast guesting - your gateway to amplifying your message, expertise, and brand! As a seasoned radio producer and podcast host with nearly three decades of experience, I'm thrilled to guide you through this transformative journey.

Podcasts offer an unparalleled platform for promoting your business, book, product, or service. It's not just free advertising; it's an opportunity to connect deeply with engaged audiences, establish your authority, and expand your reach exponentially.

Before we dive into the strategies, let's lay the groundwork for your success:

Organize for Impact

Creating a system to manage your podcast outreach is crucial. Set up a dedicated workspace and implement a method to track potential hosts, follow-ups, and interview dates. This organization will boost your booking success rate and ensure you're always prepared to shine.

Craft Your Digital Presence

Your online presence is your 24/7 ambassador. Develop a professional website or landing page that showcases your expertise, highlights your unique value proposition, and features any previous media appearances. This digital hub will be a powerful tool in convincing hosts of your guest potential.

Research and Personalize

The key to securing coveted guest spots lies in thorough research. Listen to target podcasts, understand their audience, and tailor your pitch to align with each show's specific focus. We'll explore techniques for crafting irresistible pitches that make hosts eager to feature you.

Leverage Booking Platforms

Discover how to utilize podcast booking platforms effectively. These tools can streamline your outreach process and connect you with hosts actively seeking guests like you.

Amplify Your Reach

Learn the art of crafting attention-grabbing press releases and when to consider partnering with a publicist to maximize your media exposure.

By implementing these strategies and embracing the insights shared in this guide, you'll be well-equipped to secure valuable podcast appearances.

Remember, consistency and authenticity are your greatest allies in this journey.

The podcast landscape is thriving, offering unprecedented opportunities for voices like yours to be heard. Are you ready to grab that microphone and share your story with the world?

Let's begin this exciting adventure together!

BEFORE WE GET STARTED

Congratulations on taking the first step towards sharing your expertise with the world! As we explore podcast bookings, remember that your message deserves a wide audience. Embracing diverse media opportunities can amplify your impact significantly.

If you are having questions about podcast guesting or if you'd like some professional guidance on getting booked on podcasts visit ChristineBlosdale.com for a FREE consultation.

Exploring Additional Media Avenues

While podcasts are excellent, consider these additional platforms:

Radio: Reach diverse audiences through local stations or syndicated programs.

TV: Elevate your profile through local news segments or national talk shows.

Print: Boost credibility with features in newspapers, magazines, and online publications.

Overcoming Imposter Syndrome

Imposter syndrome can hinder your success as a podcast guest. Combat it by:

- Reframing negative thoughts into positive affirmations
- Seeking support from mentors or peers
- Preparing thoroughly for appearances
- Embracing vulnerability and authenticity

Remember, your unique perspective is valuable. By implementing these strategies, you can confidently share your insights and make a lasting impact.

Embrace the Possibilities

As we begin this journey, I encourage you to explore the myriad opportunities beyond podcasts. Leverage various media platforms to amplify your message and reach diverse audiences.

In the next chapter, we'll delve into strategies for securing podcast interviews and maximizing your impact as a guest. For now, envision the exciting journey ahead – one filled with opportunities to share your wisdom and inspire others.

CRAFTING COMPELLING STORIES FOR PODCAST BOOKINGS

Mastering the art of storytelling is crucial for securing coveted podcast guest spots. This chapter explores how to craft and leverage your personal narratives to captivate hosts, connect with audiences, and stand out in the competitive world of podcast guesting.

The Power of Storytelling in Podcast Pitches

Storytelling is the secret weapon in your podcast booking arsenal. A well-crafted story can:

- Grab a host's attention in your pitch email
- Demonstrate your expertise and unique perspective
- Create an emotional connection with listeners
- Make your message memorable and shareable

Unlocking Your Signature Stories

To become a sought-after podcast guest, identify 3-5 signature stories that showcase:

1. Your journey and expertise
2. Challenges you've overcome
3. Transformative moments in your career
4. Unique insights or methodologies you've developed
5. Real-world impact of your work

Crafting Your Story Arc

Structure your stories for maximum impact:

1. Hook: Start with an intriguing opening line
2. Context: Briefly set the scene
3. Conflict: Introduce the challenge or problem
4. Climax: Describe the pivotal moment or decision
5. Resolution: Share the outcome and lessons learned

Example: "The Last Flight Out"

Here's how I've used a personal story to secure podcast bookings:

Hook: "I caught the last flight out of LA before the world shut down – all because my wife had a premonition."

Context: It was March 2020, and I had plans to travel to Australia.

Conflict: My wife sensed danger and begged me to reconsider, but I dismissed her concerns.

Climax: Suddenly, borders were closing. I had to make a split-second decision to board the final flight home or risk being separated indefinitely.

Resolution: Trusting my wife's intuition saved me from being stranded and taught me the power of listening to loved ones.

Tips for Effective Storytelling in Podcast Pitches

1. Keep it concise: Aim for 2-3 paragraphs in your initial pitch
2. Highlight relevance: Connect your story to the podcast's theme
3. Tease value: Hint at the insights listeners will gain
4. Be authentic: Share genuine emotions and vulnerabilities
5. Practice: Refine your delivery for live interviews

Leveraging Stories Across Platforms

While focusing on podcasts, remember that compelling stories can open doors to other media opportunities. Adapt your signature stories for:

- Radio interviews
- TV appearances
- Print and online articles
- Speaking engagements

Authenticity: Your Greatest Asset

As you craft your stories, prioritize authenticity. Genuine, relatable narratives will resonate with both podcast hosts and listeners, establishing you as a trustworthy and engaging guest.

Action Step: Identify your top 3 signature stories and practice pitching them in 2-3 compelling paragraphs. In the next chapter, we'll explore how to tailor these stories to specific podcasts and craft irresistible pitch emails.

YOUR TICKET TO GUESTING ON PODCASTS? YOUR SUPERPOWERS!

In the dynamic world of podcasting, securing guest spots is about showcasing your unique superpowers. Podcast hosts seek guests who bring something special to their audience and add value to their content.

Here's how to leverage your superpowers to land coveted guest spots:

Identify Your Superpowers

Reflect on what sets you apart. Are you a captivating storyteller? A subject matter expert with a fresh perspective? A natural conversationalist? Whatever your superpower, own it and understand how it can benefit podcast audiences.

Craft Your Pitch

Tailor your pitch to highlight your unique abilities. Focus on how you can enhance the podcast experience for both the host and their audience. Paint a vivid picture of what you bring to the table.

Demonstrate Your Value

Provide tangible examples of how your superpowers have made a difference. Share success stories or specific instances where you've delivered meaningful content. Showcase your track record to instill confidence in hosts.

Be Authentic and Relatable

Let your personality shine through. Be genuine and don't try to be someone you're not. Share personal anecdotes and insights that make you memorable to hosts and listeners alike.

Follow Up with Gratitude

After pitching, express sincere gratitude, regardless of the outcome. Thank hosts for considering you and reaffirm your enthusiasm. Building genuine connections can lead to future opportunities.

Remember, in the realm of audio storytelling, it's not about appearances—it's about the energy you exude and the authenticity you bring.

Whether your superpower lies in creating content, humor, negotiation, or problem-solving, recognize and embrace it fully.

Superpowers are only truly powerful when put into action. Don't be afraid to showcase your strengths and let your light shine brightly.

Own your uniqueness and let it propel you forward. The world is waiting to hear your story, and your superpowers are the key to unlocking its full potential.

REVIEWS AND TESTIMONIALS

In the competitive landscape of podcast guesting, establishing credibility and trust is paramount.

Testimonials—authentic endorsements from satisfied clients and colleagues—serve as powerful social proof, validating your expertise and impact.

Why Reviews and Testimonials Matter

- Provide tangible evidence of your expertise and professionalism
- Instill confidence in prospective clients and podcast hosts
- Showcase the real-world impact of your work

Obtaining Quality Reviews and Testimonials

1. Request feedback after each interaction or engagement
2. Ask specific questions about value received and overall satisfaction
3. Encourage written or video testimonials for added impact

Showcasing Your Endorsements

- Strategically display testimonials on your website, social media, and marketing materials
- Highlight quotes that resonate with your target audience
- Incorporate video testimonials for enhanced authenticity

Building Trust and Credibility

Leveraging testimonials in your marketing strategy:
- Attracts more clients
- Secures guest spots on podcasts
- Establishes you as a respected authority in your niche

Why Podcasters Need To See Your Reviews and Testimonials

1. Social Currency: Illustrate your ability to deliver valuable insights and engage audiences
2. Narrative of Impact: Showcase your resonance within your industry or niche
3. Tangible Benefits: Highlight your potential to captivate listeners and enhance podcast quality

Testimonials offer hosts a glimpse into:

- Your expertise in fostering engaging conversations
- Unique insights that spark profound discussions
- Potential to elevate the overall quality of their show

By strategically leveraging endorsements, you:

- Differentiate yourself from competitors
- Position yourself as an indispensable asset to podcast hosts
- Increase your chances of securing coveted guest spots

Remember, let the words of your satisfied clients speak volumes about the value you provide. Harness the power of testimonials to unlock new opportunities in the podcasting world.

THE IMPORTANCE OF A GREAT HEADSHOT

In the competitive world of media bookings, a stellar headshot is your visual calling card. It encapsulates your essence, credibility, and professionalism in a single image, making it crucial for securing guest spots on podcasts, radio shows, television appearances, or print features.

Why Your Headshot Matters:

First Impressions: A compelling headshot can be the difference-maker in catching the attention of hosts, producers, or editors.

Visual Branding: It serves as the face of your brand across all platforms.

Versatility: Many podcasts now have video versions, making a professional headshot essential for visual media.

Success Story: Julia Loggins

My client Julia Loggins transformed her branding strategy with the right headshot:

- Chose a vibrant image showcasing her among fresh produce

- Elevated her personal brand and product promotion
- Resulted in increased podcast appearances and soaring product sales
- Boosted her social media presence on Facebook, Instagram, and TikTok

Key Benefits of a Quality Headshot:
Builds Trust and Credibility: Conveys professionalism and reliability

Consistent Brand Identity: Reinforces brand recognition across all touchpoints

Humanizes Your Brand: Fosters connection and relatability with your audience

Versatile Marketing Asset: Can be repurposed across various marketing channels

Remember, your headshot is an investment in your professional image and a powerful tool for landing coveted media opportunities. It communicates that you're serious, prepared, and worthy of an audience's attention.

Don't underestimate its impact – it could be the key to unlocking doors to your success.

TOOLS AND RESOURCES

Securing podcast guest spots is achievable with a proactive approach. Here are some valuable resources and strategies to help you on your journey:

Dedicated Platforms:

PodcastGuests.com
Matchmaker.fm

These user-friendly websites connect guests with podcast hosts, allowing you to explore shows and pitch yourself directly.

Key Tips:

Listen to a few episodes before pitching to ensure alignment with the show's content and audience.

Craft personalized, informed pitches highlighting your value to the podcast.

Additional Resources:

Podcast Directories
Apple Podcasts
Spotify
Google Podcasts

Browse categories and use keyword searches to find relevant shows.

Social Media Platforms
LinkedIn
Twitter
Facebook
Engage with podcasters, participate in discussions, and showcase your expertise.

Networking Events and Conferences
Attend industry events to forge connections with hosts and professionals.

Podcast Pitching Services
Consider agencies that specialize in connecting guests with hosts.

Leverage Existing Connections

Reach out to colleagues or mentors who have appeared on podcasts for referrals.

Strategies for Success:

Tailor your pitches to each podcast

Demonstrate your unique value proposition

Maintain professionalism and persistence in your outreach

By diversifying your approach and utilizing these resources, you'll increase your chances of becoming a sought-after podcast guest.

Remember, personalized and informed pitches are far more effective than generic requests. With the right strategy, you'll be well on your way to sharing your expertise with new audiences.

CREATE YOUR VERY OWN PODCAST!

Creating your own podcast can be a game-changer for landing guest spots on other shows and amplifying your brand.

Here's why it's worth considering:

Benefits of Starting Your Own Podcast:

Showcase Expertise: Demonstrate your knowledge and insights on your own platform.

Control Content: Tailor the show to your strengths and interests.

Amplify Your Voice: Proactively share your message with a wider audience.

Build Credibility: Establish authority in your niche.

Simplicity: With the right guidance, even those with limited technical skills can succeed.

Additional Advantages:
Establish Authority: Position yourself as a thought leader in your field.

Build Personal Brand: Craft a unique identity that resonates with your audience.

Expand Network: Connect with industry leaders and influencers.

Enhance Communication Skills: Refine your storytelling and presentation abilities.

Increase Visibility: Reach a broader audience across different platforms.

Monetization Opportunities: Explore revenue generation through sponsorships, advertising, etc.

Getting Started:

Break down the process into manageable steps.
Leverage user-friendly tools and platforms.
Consider seeking guidance from a podcast coach.

Success Stories:

I've coached individuals of all ages and backgrounds, including technophobes in their 70s and 80s, who have created thriving podcasts and YouTube channels.

If you're ready to start your own podcast and would like personalized guidance, I offer private coaching services.

Contact me at ChristineBlosdale.com for a FREE consultation and take the first step towards sharing your message with the world.

Remember, creating a podcast is not just about broadcasting; it's about building connections, establishing authority, and opening doors to new opportunities in your professional journey.

HAVE A PROFESSIONAL WEBSITE

Having a professional website is indispensable in today's digital age, especially for individuals seeking to land a guest spot on a podcast.

Whether you're aiming to become a guest on talk shows, radio programs, podcasts, or be quoted in magazines, a well-designed website serves as your digital hub, allowing you to showcase your expertise, accomplishments, and offerings effectively.

One of the primary benefits of having a website is the opportunity to provide a seamless and accessible platform for people to learn more about you and your work.

By featuring your best assets, such as testimonials, portfolio, and services, you can build credibility and trust with your audience. A professional website not only serves as a virtual storefront but also reinforces your brand identity and positions you as an authority in your field.

Moreover, a website offers a centralized location for you to drive traffic and facilitate conversions. Whether it's promoting your latest book, driving sign-ups for your newsletter, or inviting visitors to explore your podcast, a website enables you to incorporate clear and compelling calls-to-action.

By directing listeners or readers to your website during media appearances, you provide them with a direct path to engage further with your content and offerings, ultimately increasing the likelihood of conversion.

Furthermore, a website serves as a dynamic tool for showcasing your versatility and expanding your reach. Beyond listing your products and services, you can leverage your website to host resources, blog posts, or video content that demonstrate your expertise and resonate with your target audience.

This multifaceted approach not only enhances your online visibility but also fosters deeper connections with your audience, positioning you as a valuable resource and thought leader in your niche.

In essence, a professional website is not just a digital presence but a strategic asset that empowers you to amplify your message, attract new opportunities, and cultivate lasting relationships with your audience.

When creating a website to appeal to podcasters and media outlets for potential guest bookings, it's essential to include specific elements that showcase your expertise, credibility, and personality.

Here are some key components to consider:

About Page:

Provide a concise yet comprehensive overview of who you are, your background, expertise, and what sets you apart. Include details about your professional journey, relevant qualifications, and any notable achievements. Highlight your unique story and what motivates you in your field.

Media Kit or Press Page:

Dedicate a section of your website to a media kit or press page, where podcasters can easily access essential information and resources about you. Include high-resolution photos, a professional bio, links to previous media appearances or interviews, and any relevant press coverage. This section should serve as a one-stop-shop for podcasters to gather information about you for potential bookings.

Speaking Topics or Expertise:

Outline the topics you are knowledgeable and passionate about, along with any speaking engagements you've had in the past. Provide brief descriptions of each topic or area of expertise, showcasing your ability to deliver valuable insights and engaging content to podcast audiences.

This section helps podcasters understand the value you can bring to their show and aligns your expertise with their audience's interests.

Testimonials and Social Proof:

Incorporate testimonials from previous podcast hosts, clients, or industry peers who can vouch for your expertise and credibility as a guest. Include their feedback and endorsements prominently on your website to build trust and credibility with potential podcasters.

Additionally, display social proof such as follower counts, audience metrics, or endorsements from influential figures in your industry.

Contact Information and Booking Form:

Make it easy for podcasters to reach out to you by providing clear contact information or a booking form directly on your website. Include a dedicated section where podcast hosts can inquire about potential collaborations, interviews, or speaking engagements.

Ensure that your contact details are easily accessible and prominently displayed on every page of your website.

By including these elements on your website, you can effectively position yourself as an attractive and compelling guest for podcasters seeking knowledgeable and engaging experts to feature on their shows.

IT'S TIME TO GET SOCIAL!

In today's digital age, being active on social media is essential for professionals aiming to secure guest spots on podcasts and establish themselves as authorities in their industry.

Social media platforms offer a powerful opportunity to showcase your knowledge, skills, and personality while connecting with a global audience.

For individuals seeking to land more bookings as guests on podcasts, maintaining an active and engaging presence on social media can significantly enhance their credibility and visibility within their industry.

In today's digital landscape, a strong social media presence is crucial for landing podcast guest spots and establishing industry authority.

Here's how to leverage social media effectively:

1. Showcase Expertise
- Share valuable content consistently
- Offer insights, tips, and personal anecdotes
- Position yourself as a thought leader

2. Build a Following
- Cultivate an engaged audience
- Demonstrate your influence to podcast hosts

3. Network Strategically
- Connect with podcast hosts and influencers
- Engage in relevant conversations
- Stay top-of-mind for guest opportunities

Platform-Specific Strategies:

Facebook:
- Utilize groups for discussions
- Share informative content
- Host Facebook Live Q&As

Instagram:
- Create visually appealing posts
- Use relevant hashtags
- Leverage Stories and Reels

TikTok:
- Create educational short-form videos
- Participate in trends
- Collaborate with other creators

YouTube:
- Host longer-form content
- Optimize for discoverability
- Engage through comments and live streams

LinkedIn:
- Share industry insights
- Participate in professional groups
- Publish long-form articles

Stand Out with:
- Interactive content (polls, quizzes)
- User-generated content
- Visual storytelling
- Influencer collaborations
- Behind-the-scenes glimpses
- Consistent value provision

Remember: Authenticity, consistency, and value-driven content are key to attracting podcast hosts and securing guest spots.

Leverage each platform's unique features to showcase your expertise and engage your audience effectively.

RESOURCES TO HELP YOU GET BOOKED

To excel as a podcast guest and secure media features, leverage these key strategies:

1. Define Your Brand and Expertise
   - Identify your unique selling points
   - Pinpoint your areas of knowledge and passion
   -

2. Know Your Target Audience
   - Tailor your messaging to resonate with your ideal listeners

3. Choose the Right Mediums
   - Align with your strengths (speaking, writing, etc.)

4. Utilize Media Opportunity Resources
   - Connectively (formerly HARO): Respond to journalist queries
   - SourceBottle: Connect with media seeking expert sources

5. Craft Compelling Pitches
   - Highlight your expertise and relevance
   - Tailor to each opportunity

Sample Pitch Template:

"Hello [Podcaster's Name],
I was captivated by your discussions on [topic]. With [X] years in [field], I've [significant accomplishment]. My perspective on [topic] could offer valuable insights to your audience.

I'd love to share my expertise on your show. Open to exploring this further?

Best regards,
[Your Name]"

6. Build Media Relationships
- Engage with content on social media
- Attend networking events
- Personalize your outreach

Pro Tips:
- Stay proactive and consistent in your efforts
- Maintain authenticity in all interactions
- Follow up professionally after appearances

By implementing these strategies, you'll position yourself as an industry expert and increase your visibility through podcast appearances and media features.

Remember, success in the media landscape comes from a combination of expertise, strategic outreach, and genuine relationship-building.

THE POSSIBILITIES ARE ENDLESS!

Podcasting has emerged as a powerful platform for experts to share knowledge and insights with global audiences.

The opportunities for podcast guesting are virtually limitless, offering numerous benefits:

Reach Diverse Audiences: Connect with engaged listeners receptive to your expertise.

Boost Credibility: Enhance your professional reputation by appearing on respected shows.

Expand Your Network: Forge valuable connections with hosts, guests, and industry leaders.

Attract Media Attention: Showcase your expertise to journalists and media outlets.

Unlock New Opportunities: Open doors to speaking engagements, consulting gigs, and collaborations.

Examples of Potential Outcomes:

Increased visibility and authority in your field

Invitations to speak at conferences or events

Media features in articles or TV segments

Book deals or publishing opportunities

Consulting and coaching requests

Brand partnerships and sponsorships

Community engagement and impact

By leveraging podcast appearances, experts can elevate their profile, expand their influence, and create lasting opportunities for professional growth.

As the podcasting landscape evolves, those who embrace this platform can unlock endless possibilities for success in their field.

Remember, each podcast appearance is a chance to showcase your unique perspective and expertise.

By consistently delivering value to listeners, you'll maximize the potential benefits and opportunities that arise from your podcast guesting journey.

EXPERT GUIDANCE: THE ROLE OF A COACH

In today's dynamic media landscape, securing coveted spots on podcasts, radio shows, and local television programs can significantly amplify your message and boost your success.

As an entrepreneur, author, coach, or thought leader, you have a unique story to tell – but how do you ensure it reaches the right audience?

This is where the expertise of a media coach becomes invaluable. With over 25 years of experience helping clients worldwide expand their brand and business, I've witnessed firsthand the transformative power of expert guidance in navigating the media landscape.

A media coach offers:

Insider Knowledge: Understand the intricacies of pitching, interviewing, and audience engagement.

Personalized Strategy: Tailor your approach to highlight your unique value proposition.

Confidence Building: Overcome fears and approach media opportunities with purpose.

Industry Connections: Leverage extensive networks to open doors.

Long-term Growth: Invest in skills that continually attract

new opportunities.

Ready to Unlock Your Podcast Guesting Potential?

Imagine confidently sharing your expertise on top-rated podcasts, engaging with radio audiences, or captivating viewers on local TV. These aren't just dreams – they're achievable goals with the right guidance.

I invite you to take the next step in your media journey. Just book a FREE consultation with me at ChatWithChristineB.com.

Let's explore how we can transform your expertise into compelling media appearances that grow your brand and business.

For a comprehensive look at all my coaching programs, including rave testimonials from successful clients, visit ChristineBlosdale.com.

Discover how my range of services – from private coaching to podcast production and social media marketing – can propel your success.

Don't let another opportunity pass you by. Your message deserves to be heard. Let's work together to make it resonate across the media landscape.

Book your FREE consultation today and let's start crafting your media success story!

ADDITIONAL SERVICES AVAILABLE AT

CHRISTINEBLOSDALE.COM

• Private and Group Media and Business Coaching

• Podcast, Radio and YouTube Channel Development and Production

• Social Media Marketing

• Event Emcee & Public Speaking

• Promotional and Branding Video Production

• Website & Social Media Consultation

• Professional Voice Over and Narration

www.ingramcontent.com/pod-product-compliance
Lightning Source LLC
LaVergne TN
LVHW051750050326
832903LV00029B/2841